Explore the Maya Civilization

Zelda Wagner

Lerner Publications ◆ Minneapolis

Lerner Publications Company
An imprint of Lerner Publishing Group, Inc.
241 First Avenue North
Minneapolis, MN 55401 USA

For reading levels and more information, look up this title at www.lernerbooks.com.

Main body text set in Billy Infant Regular. Typeface provided by SparkyType.

Editor: Evan Villas **Photo Editor:** Lucien Brinkley
Lerner team: Sue Marquis

Library of Congress Cataloging-in-Publication Data

Names: Wagner, Zelda, 2000- author
Title: Explore the Maya civilization / Zelda Wagner.
Description: Minneapolis : Lerner Publications, [2026] | Series: Lightning bolt books : Early civilizations | Includes bibliographical references and index. | Audience: Ages 6-9 | Audience: Grades 2-3 | Summary: "Over one thousand years ago, the Maya people thrived in Mesoamerica. Readers uncover the Maya way of life—what they ate, the clothes they wore, the gods they worshipped, and how their civilization vanished"— Provided by publisher.
Identifiers: LCCN 2025011871 (print) | LCCN 2025011872 (ebook) | ISBN 9798765689257 lib. bdg. | ISBN 9798348028947 pbk | ISBN 9798765696705 epub
Subjects: LCSH: Mayas—Social life and customs—Juvenile literature | Central America—Civilization—Juvenile literature | Mexico—Civilization—Juvenile literature
Classification: LCC F1435.3.S7 W34 2026 (print) | LCC F1435.3.S7 (ebook) | DDC 972.81—dc23/eng/20250606

LC record available at https://lccn.loc.gov/2025011871
LC ebook record available at https://lccn.loc.gov/2025011872

Manufactured in the United States of America
1-1012502-54793-5/1/2025

Table of Contents

The Ancient Maya

Maya civilization began around four thousand years ago in Mesoamerica. This region includes Central America and southern Mexico.

The Maya lived in the jungle. They learned to use plants and animals for food and medicine.

The Maya built huge temples in the jungle.

Maya civilization was divided into city-states. They were connected by roads.

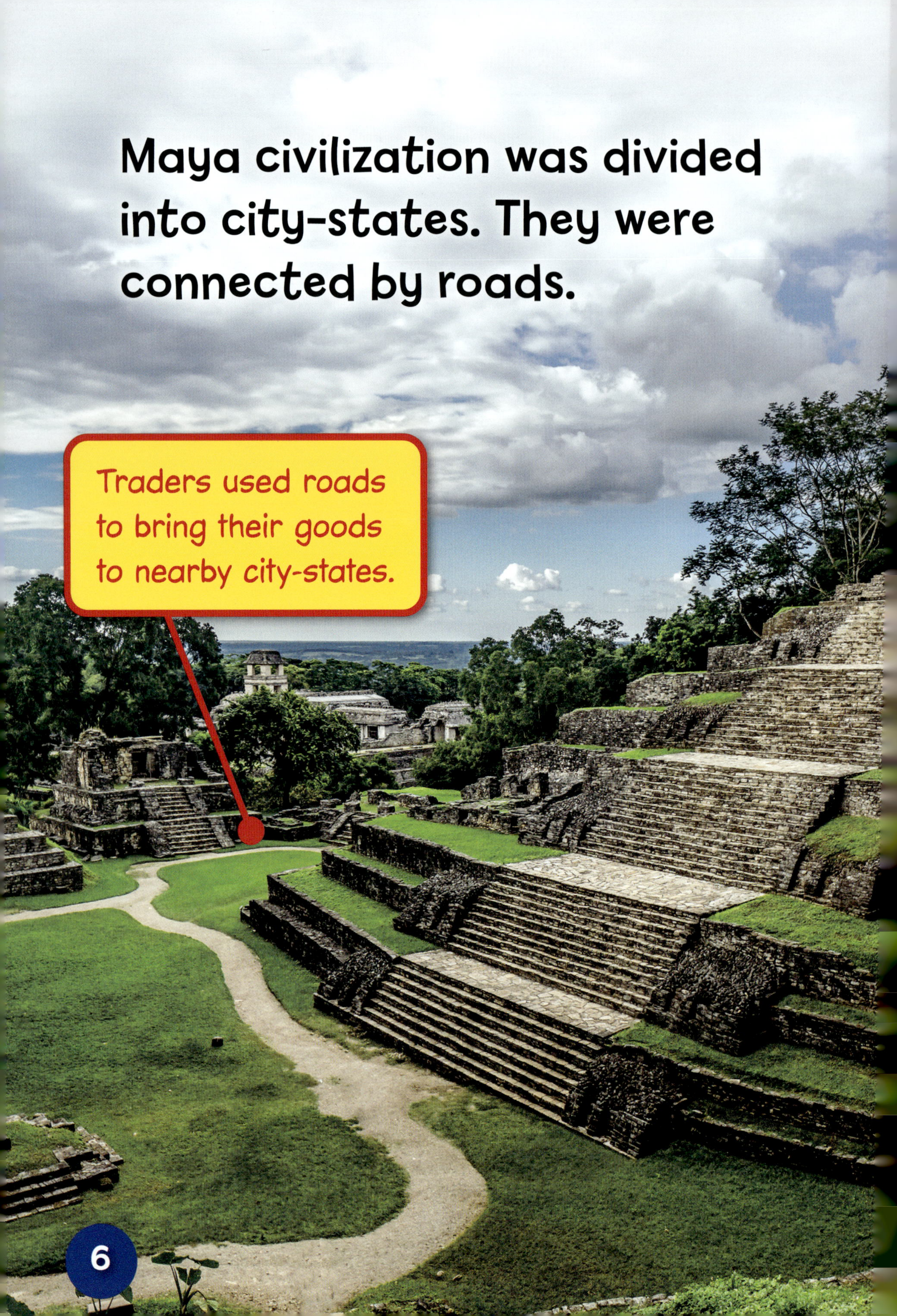

Maya calendars helped people plan harvests and religious ceremonies.

The Maya honored their gods and studied astronomy. **They created calendars that stretched far into the future.**

The Maya grew crops such as maize and beans. They hunted deer and turkeys for meat.

Maize is another word for *corn.*

Maya Civilization
Ancient Maya Civilization
City
GULF OF MEXICO
Chichén Itzá
MEXICO
CARIBBEAN SEA
CENTRAL AMERICA
PACIFIC OCEAN

Maya Life

How the Maya lived depended on their class, or social rank. Enslaved people lived the hardest lives. They were often enemies who were captured in battle.

Farmers grew food. Craftspeople made stone tools and colorful clothing. They also made jewelry, masks, and figures out of jade.

Nobles were the highest class. They ruled over city-states. Each city-state also had a king.

Nobles wore large, colorful headdresses made from cloth, jade, and animal feathers.

Priests decided when it was time to plant crops.

Priests were another powerful class. They made decisions for Maya society. They oversaw huge temples.

Temples were shaped like pyramids. Food, drinks, and animals were given as offerings to Maya gods. Sometimes humans were sacrificed to keep the gods happy.

This temple at Chichén Itzá was an important Maya site for thousands of years.

A Maya book

The Maya wrote with pictures. Some pictures stood for a specific sound. The Maya made colorful, folding books.

Modern-day relatives of the Maya still play Maya games.

A ball game was popular among the Maya. Each team worked to hit a small ball through a stone ring. Sometimes the losers were sacrificed to the gods.

The Fall of the Maya

About a thousand years ago, many Maya cities were deserted. No one knows exactly why.

Scientists think that Mesoamerica had a long drought around this time. Crops may have failed. The large cities may not have had enough food.

A corn field destroyed by drought

Millions of people today are related to the Maya.

Some Maya cities lasted until the Spanish colonized the region five hundred years ago. This was the true end of the ancient Maya.

A Look at the Maya Creation Story

One Maya story explains how the gods created the world. It says the world started in darkness. Then the god Huracán made light appear. Next, the gods of nature made plants and animals. But they wanted more. After many failed attempts, the gods made humans out of corn dough. These were said to be the first modern people.

Maya Facts

- Some Maya nobles had tattoos. They often depicted animals or gods.
- Maya temples were built to line up with the sun, the moon, or planets and stars.
- The Maya used cocoa beans as money.
- The Maya were one of the first civilizations to use the number zero.

Glossary

astronomy: the study of the sun, moon, stars, and other objects in outer space

city-state: a self-governing city and the lands it controls

civilization: a large society in which people share a common government and culture

colonize: to take over a land by force

drought: when it doesn't rain for a long period of time

jade: a type of green gemstone

offering: something that is given to honor a god

sacrifice: to kill an animal or person as an offering to a god

temple: a building that is used to worship a god or gods

Learn More

BBC Bitesize: An Introduction to the Ancient Maya
https://www.bbc.co.uk/bitesize/articles/zqv6msg

Britannica Kids: Maya
https://kids.britannica.com/kids/article/Maya/353445

Dittmer, Lori. *Chichén Itzá*. Creative Education, 2025.

Faust, D. R. *The Rise and Fall of the Maya Civilization*. Bearport, 2025.

Havemeyer, Janie. *A Day in Ancient Maya*. Jump!, 2025.

Kiddle: Mayan Civilization Facts for Kids
https://kids.kiddle.co/Mayan_civilization

Index

Photo Acknowledgments

Image credits: Adalberto Rios Szalay/Sexto Sol/Getty Images, p. 4; THEPALMER/Getty Images, p. 5; Diego Grandi/Shutterstock, p. 6; AlevtinaGorskaya/Shutterstock, p. 7; KarlosVBrito7/Getty Images, p. 8; Laura Westlund/Independent Picture Service, p. 9; mofles/Getty Images, p. 10; Sepia Times/Universal Images Group via Getty Images, p. 11; Science History Images/Alamy, p. 12; Reimar/Shutterstock, p. 13; © Marco Bottigelli/Getty Images, p. 14; Dresden Codex, circa 1200, p. 15; Cavan Images/Alamy, p. 16; Alberto Expósito Pérez/Getty Images, p. 17; Marccophoto/Getty Images, p. 18; Gaetan Mariage/Alamy, p. 19; photography by p. lubas/Getty Images, p. 20.

Cover: Panther Media GmbH/Alamy.